MY FIRST
BIBLE

Stories by Lizzie Ribbons
Illustrations by Paola Bertolini Grudina

This book belongs to

....

A gift from

....

On the occasion of your Special Day

at

....

....

on this date

....

Father God, Creator of all that is good,
thank you for the gift of this precious child,
the miracle of this special baby,
the wonder of new life
and the mystery of human love.

"Children are a blessing and a gift from the Lord."
Psalm 127:3, CEV

My name is ....

....

I was born on ....

I weighed ....

My eyes are...

My hair is ....

I live at this address ....

....

....

....

My grandfather's name

....

My grandfather's date and place of birth

....

....

....

My grandmother's name

....

My grandmother's date and place of birth

....

....

....

My father's name

....

My father's date and place of birth

....

....

....

8

My grandmother's name

....

My grandmother's date and place of birth

....

....

My grandfather's name

....

My grandfather's date and place of birth

....

....

....

My mother's name

....

My mother's date and place of birth

....

....

....

My name

....

....

....

My Family

O God, your generous love surrounds us
and everything we enjoy comes from you.

*

Lord, bless us and protect us.
Lord, smile on us and show us your love.
Lord, help us and take care of us.
Lord, guide us, keep us and grant us your peace.

My Progress

I first smiled ....

I cut my first tooth ....

I first sat up ....

I first crawled ....

My first words ....

I first walked ....

My favourite things ....

....

....

Bible Stories and Prayers

PRAYERS

God made the world

Long ago, at the beginning of time, God said, 'Let there be light,' and bright light shone in the darkness. God said, 'Let there be land and sea,' and land filled with mountains appeared, surrounded by deep water. God said, 'Let there be trees and plants, sun, moon and stars,' and the plants produced fruit in the sunshine and were cool under the moon and stars.

God said, 'Let there be fish and winged creatures,' and the sea teemed with fish and the sky was filled with birds and butterflies.

God said, 'Let there be all kinds of animals,' and tigers padded and antelope galloped over the land.

God said, 'Let there be people to look after my beautiful world,' and there were, male and female. God saw that his world was good and he rested.

Noah builds an ark

God told Noah to build an ark. Soon there would be a flood that would cover the earth.

Noah built an ark, a very, very big boat, and took his family and all the animals, two by two, inside.

Then it began to rain, splish, splash, splish, splash.

The water covered the ground, the trees and even the mountain tops, but Noah and his family and all the animals were safe inside.

Days passed and nights passed before the rain stopped.

Only when a dove came back carrying an olive leaf did Noah know that soon it would be safe for them to leave the ark.

Then God sent a beautiful rainbow.

'There will never be a flood like this again,' God promised.

Under the stars

Avery long time ago, a rich man called Abraham lived in a big city called Ur.

God told Abraham to move house and go from place to place, living in a tent, until God gave him a new home in a new country.

Abraham trusted God. He took with him his wife, Sarah, and his nephew, Lot. He took his servants and his sheep and his goats.

'Come and look at the stars,' God said to Abraham one dark and twinkly night. 'You are just the beginning. There will be many, many people in your family. There will be many, many children born to the people in your family. There will be as many in your family as there are stars in the sky.'

Abraham had no children. He and Sarah were getting old. But Abraham knew God. He knew that God always keeps his promises.

Three visitors

One hot day, three visitors came to Abraham as he rested in the shade.

'Here's water for washing and drinking,' said Abraham. 'Come and rest and eat.'

Sarah cooked her very best food and Abraham served it to them under the shady trees.

Sarah stayed in the tent and listened as the men talked.

'Soon Sarah will give birth to your baby son,' said one of the men to Abraham.

'I'm much too old to have a baby!' Sarah laughed to herself. 'I'm old enough to be a grandma!'

'Nothing is too hard for God to do,' said the man. 'You wait and see.'

Then Abraham knew that God had sent the men with a message for him. So they waited and they trusted God, and soon Sarah's baby boy was born. They called him Isaac.

Isaac and Rebekah

Abraham loved his son, but when Isaac was older, his father wanted to find a good wife for him to marry. He sent his servant on a long journey back to his home country to find someone who would love him and take care of him.

When they stopped by a well, the servant asked God to send a girl who would be kind enough to bring water for him and for his ten thirsty camels!

'Would you like some water?' a beautiful girl asked him. 'Can I get water for your camels too?'

God had answered the servant's prayer. Rebekah was the granddaughter of Abraham's brother. The family welcomed him and listened as he explained why he had come.

The servant took Rebekah back with him. Isaac knew that he loved her and wanted her to be his wife.

Joseph and his brothers

Jacob was one of Isaac's sons and Joseph was one of Jacob's sons. Jacob loved Joseph the best and gave him a beautiful coat to wear.

'That's not fair,' his eleven brothers said.

One day Joseph dreamed about the sun and the moon and eleven stars. They all bowed down to him! He dreamed about bundles of corn that his brothers had grown. They all bowed down to Joseph's own bundle of corn.

'So you think you're special?' muttered his brothers. 'You think we'll bow down to you, do you?'

They were so angry that they threw Joseph into a deep, dark pit. Then they sold him to some traders who were going far away to Egypt.

They told Jacob that a wild animal had killed him!
But God looked after Joseph. He worked hard for a kind
master. Then, because he was put in prison, he got to meet
the king of Egypt…

Dreams come true

The king of Egypt had dreamed strange dreams. He was told that Joseph could help him.

'I saw seven thin cows eat seven fat cows!' said the

king. 'I saw seven dry ears of corn eat seven plump ears of corn!'

'Seven years of good harvests will be followed by seven years with nothing at all!' said Joseph. 'God is warning you about the future.'

The king made Joseph a great man in his kingdom so that he could store the corn to help the people when none would grow.

Back in Canaan, Joseph's family were very hungry indeed. So Jacob sent his sons to buy corn in Egypt.

When Joseph saw his brothers he remembered the horrible things they had done to him but he also knew how much he had missed them. He knew that God had made everything good again.

'Look, it's me!' said Joseph. 'Bring my father here too, so we can all live here together in Egypt.'

The baby in the basket

Baby Moses was crying – loudly.

His mother was so afraid that the king's soldiers would hear him that she hid him. She wove some reeds together and made a basket for him. She floated the basket on the River Nile with baby Moses inside.

Since Joseph's time long ago, thousands of God's people had come to live in Egypt. The new king had made them all his slaves. He was afraid that all the little baby boys would grow up into men who might fight him, so he tried to kill them all.

Big sister Miriam hid in the reeds and watched her baby brother bobbing about in the basket.

And who should come along but the king's own daughter!

'Oh!' said the princess. 'What a sweet baby. I'll look after you!'

'I know someone who can help you…' said Miriam, popping up. And she fetched her mother, Moses' mother!

Now everyone was happy. And God had kept baby Moses safe.

The king who said 'No!'

When Moses was grown up, God spoke to him from a bright and blazing bush.

'Moses, you are going to lead my people out of Egypt to a better place,' said God.

'But I can't! I don't know how,' Moses said.

'Yes, you can,' said God. 'You can do anything if I help you.'

Now the king of Egypt had made God's people his slaves.

'Let my people go,' Moses said to the king of Egypt.

But the king said 'No!'

So the rivers went muddy. Then there were frogs and gnats and flies everywhere, hopping and buzzing. The animals and people became ill. Huge hailstones rained down from the dark sky and clouds of insects chomped at the crops until the ground was bare.

'Let my people go!' Moses said to the king of Egypt.

But still the king said 'No!'

Finally, when lots of people had died, the king changed his mind.

'Go, go, GO!' said the king of Egypt.

Follow-my-leader

Moses led God's people out of Egypt. Every day, a tall cloud showed them where to go. Every night, a tall fire showed them where to rest.

When they reached the Red Sea, Moses lifted his stick and the wind blew a path across the sea so everyone could cross over on dry land.

God provided food when the people were hungry. He provided water when they were thirsty. The people grumbled but they followed Moses day by day and Moses followed God day by day.

One day Moses talked with God high on a mountain. When he came down the mountain, he brought with him ten special rules to help his people live together happily.

The best way to live

'I am the true and living God,' God had said. 'Don't worship anyone else.

'Don't worship pictures or statues of other gods.

'Use my name when you talk to me and treat it with respect.

'Rest on the seventh day of the week – make it a happy day, a holy day, when everyone can worship me together.

'Look after your mums and dads and love them always.

'Don't hurt anyone; don't even think about hurting them.

'Don't steal someone else's wife or husband and treat them as if they are your own.

'Don't steal anything that belongs to someone else.

'Don't tell lies or say nasty things about other people.

'Don't look at the things other people have and want them so much that you can't think about anything else.'

'We must love God and be kind to each other,' said Moses. 'This is the best way to live and be happy.'

Walls come tumbling down

When Moses died, Joshua became the new leader of God's people.

'Don't be afraid, Joshua,' said God. 'Trust me and I will help you.'

God was going to lead his people into a beautiful land. But first they had to cross the River Jordan – wide and fast and deep and dangerous.

'Don't be afraid,' Joshua told the people. 'Trust God and he will help us.'

As the priests stepped into the river, the water dried up! Everyone crossed safely to the other side.

Then they had to get past the walls of Jericho – tall and thick and high and wide.

'Don't be afraid,' said Joshua. 'Trust God and he will help us.'

Joshua's soldiers did lots of marching around the city walls and the priests did lots of blowing on trumpets and the people did lots of shouting… and the walls of the city fell down!

Then Joshua and God's people lived in Canaan, the land that God had promised them.

Gideon's sign from God

Gideon was hiding from the Midianites. They swept down on their camels and took all the food that God's people were growing.

'Hello, you strong, brave man!' said an angel one day. 'God wants you to help his people.'

Gideon looked around him. Surely the angel wasn't talking to him?

'People have forgotten the rules God gave them,' said the angel. 'God wants you to help them remember them again.'

'But I am not big or clever or special and my family is not big or clever or special… Are you sure God wants me to help?'

So God showed Gideon that he did. One day Gideon left a sheep's fleece on the ground. God made it wet when the ground around it was dry.

The next day he made the sheep's fleece dry when the ground around it was wet with dew.

Then Gideon knew that God could do anything! And that God had chosen him to help his people.

Gideon trusted God – and God helped them all to live in peace again.

Ruth in the cornfield

Lots of sad, bad things had happened to Naomi but God was kind and good. He sent Ruth to take care of her.

'Lots of sad, bad things have happened,' said Ruth, 'but I will go with you to Bethlehem and look after you, and I will love your God.'

Ruth worked in the cornfield. God was kind and good to her. He sent Boaz to make sure she had enough food to take home to Naomi.

'God is kind and good!' said Naomi. 'First he sent Ruth to take care of me and now he has sent Boaz to take care of us both!'

After a while Boaz married Ruth and they were very happy together. They had a baby boy called Obed.

'God is kind and good!' said Naomi. 'First he gave me Ruth and then he sent Boaz to take care of us both. Now he has made us one big family to take care of each other!'

The voice in the night

Hannah wanted a baby very much.

'Please help me,' Hannah prayed to God. 'I do so want a baby and any child I have will be yours as well.'

God gave Hannah and her husband a baby boy. She called him Samuel and she was very happy. When Samuel was old enough, Hannah took him to the temple.

'I will teach him about God and the right way to live,' said Eli the priest. 'I will look after Samuel.'

One night Samuel woke to hear someone calling his name.

Samuel ran to old Eli.

'Here I am,' said Samuel.

'I didn't call you,' said Eli. 'Go back to bed.'

Samuel heard the voice again.

'Here I am,' said Samuel – again.
'I didn't call you,' said Eli. 'Go back to bed.'
Then Samuel heard the voice again.
This time Eli knew it was God calling Samuel.
'Tell God you're listening to him,' said Eli.
'I'm listening, God,' said Samuel. 'I will always listen to you.'

Seven sons and a shepherd boy

Samuel helped God's people when he was grown up. He always trusted God and God helped him.

Now the people wanted a king. Samuel asked God to help him choose the right person.

Jesse brought seven of his sons to Samuel.

'Should it be the tallest and strongest?' thought

Samuel. One... two... three... four... five... six... seven. All of them were tall and strong.

Then God whispered in Samuel's ear.

'Not the tallest, not the strongest, but the person who is good and true inside.'

'Have you any other sons?' Samuel asked Jesse.

'Well, there's David,' said Jesse. 'But he's out in the fields taking care of my sheep.'

'I'll wait,' said Samuel.

When David came in, Samuel said, 'This is the boy God has chosen to be king. Not the tallest, not the strongest, but the person who is good and true inside.'

He sprinkled a few drops of oil on David's head. One day David would be king.

David and the giant

David was not as big as a soldier but Goliath was very, very big. He was huge. He was enormous. He was a GIANT!

Goliath's army stood on one side. King Saul's army stood on the other side looking very worried.

'Who will come and fight me?' Goliath shouted day after day.

He was wearing a lot of heavy armour. He looked ugly and fierce and very bad indeed. Everyone was very, very afraid of him – everyone except David.

'I'll fight him,' said David. 'God helped me fight lions and bears when I looked after my sheep. He will help me now.'

'What?' roared the giant. 'You're just a boy!'

David found five pebbles in the stream, one... two... three... four... five. He whirled one around in his shepherd's sling. Then he threw it at Goliath as hard as he could. Goliath fell to the ground. And that was the end of the big, bad giant.

King Saul's army cheered and shouted – and Goliath's army ran away!

God is my shepherd

David wrote a lot of songs. Some of his songs were happy and some were sad. Some were brave and some were bold. Some were praises and some were prayers.

David told God everything because God was his friend. David knew that God was with him when he was happy

and God was with him when he felt sad or frightened,
lonely or grumpy.

    'God is my shepherd,' David sang. 'I am his sheep.
God leads me where it's rough and steep,
or by still waters, cool and deep.
He walks beside me every day,
in all the places where I play;
in every step along the way.
I walk behind him in his light,
in the darkness shining bright;
I know I'm always in his sight.
He spreads out food and comes to greet –
"Everybody, take a seat!
Everybody, come and eat!"'

A very wise king

King Solomon was very young when he became king.

'What would you like me to give you?' asked God.

Solomon thought hard. Did he want to be rich and famous and have lots of money? Did he want to be strong and brave and live for ever? Did he want lots of things for himself?

'I would like to be good and wise, fair and just and true – a good king who rules his people well.'

God was very pleased with Solomon's answer. He made Solomon good and wise, fair and just – but he gave him lots of other good things too.

All sorts of people came to Solomon. He told them how to live a good and happy life.

Then King Solomon built a great and wonderful temple for God.

'This is a place where your people can ask you to forgive them or tell you how great you are,' said Solomon. 'But I know that you do not live in any kind of house. You are with us, God, wherever we are.'

Elijah and the ravens

'It's not going to rain for a very long time,' said Elijah to King Ahab. 'God is not at all happy with the bad things you have been doing. There won't be much to eat or drink. The earth will be dry and bare.'

'Mmmm…' said King Ahab, who wasn't sure whether to believe Elijah or not.

God told Elijah to go and stay by a little stream where he could drink clear water. Every day God sent large black ravens to Elijah with food in their beaks. Gradually Elijah's little stream dried up.

'Go now to the little village of Zarephath,' God told Elijah. 'There is a widow there who will make sure you have enough to eat.'

'It's all I have left,' the widow told Elijah. 'After this I have no more flour or oil to make bread.'

But for as long as she shared her food with Elijah, God made sure that the little jar of flour and the little bottle of oil did not run out.

Fire on the mountain

There was still no rain. It was time for Elijah to go back to the king.

'Let's see who is the real God – my God or the stone statue you worship,' said Elijah.

Elijah laid a fire on top of stones and the people who believed Baal the stone statue was real did the same.

'Come on, Baal!' shouted the people who worshipped the pretend god. 'Light our fire! listen to us and answer! Listen to us!'

They shouted until they were exhausted and their throats were sore. But nothing happened.

'Has Baal run away?' teased Elijah. 'Perhaps he's gone to sleep? Perhaps he's on holiday!'

Then Elijah poured water all round his fire.

'Let everyone see that you are the one true and living God,' Elijah prayed to God.

Then fire fell from heaven and the wood sizzled and burned. The people fell to their knees and worshipped God. Then God sent rain once more to the earth.

A dip in the river

A little servant girl lived in the house of an important soldier in a nearby country. She saw that her master had spots and nasty sore places all over his skin. She told his wife that God could help him.

So Naaman sent a message to the king in the servant girl's country.

'It's no good asking me,' the king said. 'I can't make you better. But you could go and ask Elisha, the prophet.' So Naaman went to visit Elisha.

'Go and wash in the River Jordan seven times,' said Elisha's servant.

Naaman wasn't happy.

'First he sends his servant instead of seeing me himself. Then he tells me to have a bath in a dirty river! I thought he'd wave his arms, or say some prayers…!'

'Go on, Naaman,' said his servant. 'Just do it!' Grumpily, Naaman went into the river – seven times. And the spots and the sores vanished.

Naaman couldn't stop smiling. God had healed him.

Jonah runs the other way

God told Jonah to go to a city called Nineveh.

But Jonah didn't want to go. The people there were cruel and wicked. So he ran away. He sailed away in the opposite direction.

A big storm blew, and the sailors were afraid they'd all be drowned.

'Throw me into the sea!' said Jonah. 'It's all my fault! I've disobeyed God.'

'If that's what you want…' said the sailors.

Jonah fell into the water but a huge fish swallowed him up in one large swallow.

Jonah stayed inside the fish for three days and three nights. And Jonah prayed…

The huge fish spat Jonah out of its mouth onto the beach.

This time Jonah went to the city of Nineveh. He told the people there to stop doing bad things – and the people said they were sorry! So God forgave the people.

'That's why I wanted you to come,' said God. 'Now these bad people have changed their ways. That's good!'

The terrible fiery furnace

Shadrach, Meshach and Abednego were taken to be servants in the king's court far away in Babylon. One day the king told everyone to bow down and worship a golden statue.

'I won't,' said Shadrach.

'I won't,' said Meshach.

'I won't,' said Abednego.

'There'll be trouble if you don't!' said a messenger. 'As soon as you hear music and instruments, you must worship that golden statue or you'll be thrown into a fiery furnace!'

'We will only worship the one true God,' they said.

So they were thrown into the blazing fiery furnace. It was very, very, very hot.

But God sent an angel into the fiery furnace to keep them safe. Shadrach, Meshach and Abednego did not get burned. They didn't even smell smoky!

When the king brought them out of the fiery furnace, he knew that their God was the one true God!

Plots and plans and lions

Daniel was also taken to be a servant of the king in Babylon. The king's men saw he was good and wise, and they didn't like him, so they planned and plotted and then went to the king.

'You're the greatest person on earth, oh King, and everyone should pray to you. Anyone who doesn't should be thrown to the lions,' they said, bowing low.

'OK!' said the king.

Daniel knew about the new law but he prayed to God every day at his open window, just as he had before.

'Daniel still prays to God,' they said.

'Daniel likes God best,' they said.

'Daniel has broken your law,' they said.

'Daniel…'

'Enough!' said the king.

The king knew that he had to throw Daniel to the lions.

'I hope your God will save you,' he said to Daniel.

It was a long, lonely night for the king, but in the morning the king found Daniel… alive and well!

'I trusted God and he took care of me,' said Daniel.

'Daniel's God is the true and living God,' said the king. 'He is amazing!'

Mary meets an angel

Mary was an ordinary girl. But God thought she was very special indeed. God sent the angel Gabriel to see her one day.

'Don't be afraid,' said the angel. 'I have a message for you from God. You are going to have a baby. The baby will be God's own Son and Jesus will be his name.'

'But I am still young – and I don't have a husband yet,' she said.

'Don't worry, Mary,' Gabriel said. 'Nothing is too hard for God to do.'

Mary was a little afraid, but she was also very happy. She ran to tell her cousin, Elizabeth, the news.

'You are very special, Mary!' Elizabeth said. 'Everyone will know how much God has blessed you.'

'You are wise and wonderful!' Mary prayed to God. 'You're the greatest and the best!'

A long way to Bethlehem

The angel Gabriel told Joseph, the village carpenter, to marry Mary and take care of her and her baby. The baby grew inside Mary and soon the time came for her little son to be born.

But the Romans wanted to count all the people in the empire. Mary and Joseph had to travel a long way to Bethlehem. When they reached the town, it was very busy.

'No room here!' they were told, when they looked for somewhere to stay. 'But… you can rest in the stable, if you like.'

That night, Mary's baby was born, Jesus, the Son of God. Mary wrapped him up warmly and made a bed for him in the manger where the animals fed.

The shepherds' surprise

Shepherds were out on the hills that night, looking after their sheep. Suddenly there was a bright light all around them! They heard the voice of an angel!

'Don't be afraid,' said the angel. 'I have good news for you! Jesus, the Son of God, has been born in Bethlehem. You'll find him lying in a manger.'

Then many more angels appeared, singing songs of praise to God.

The shepherds knew what they must do – they must go to see the baby in the manger for themselves.

They found the baby Jesus with Mary and Joseph and told them all about the message of the angels. Then they told everyone they saw what had happened that night.

Following the star

There was a very bright star shining in the sky on the night Jesus was born. Wise men in the East saw the star and wondered what it might mean.

'It means that a new king has been born to the Jewish people,' said one.

'We must take gifts fit for a king,' said another.

'We must go to worship him,' said a third.

They made a long, long journey, following the bright
star all the way until they found the new-born king.

They knelt down in wonder and gave him their gifts
of gold, frankincense and myrrh. Then they worshipped
him – Jesus, the Son of God.

Jesus is lost

Every year, Jesus grew bigger and stronger. Every year, Jesus went to the temple in Jerusalem with Mary and Joseph and many other people for a special festival called the Passover.

When Jesus was twelve years old, something terrible happened for Mary and Joseph. They were on their way home from Jerusalem when Mary realised she hadn't seen Jesus for a while.

'Where's Jesus?' she asked.

They searched among their friends; they searched among their family. But they couldn't find Jesus anywhere!

So Mary and Joseph hurried back to Jerusalem.

It was three days before they found Jesus. He had been in the temple all the time, listening to the teachers there.

'Why were you looking for me?' Jesus said, surprised. 'Didn't you know I needed to be in my father's house – God's house – so I could learn all about him.'

Jesus went home with Mary and Joseph. He grew taller and stronger, and went on learning about God.

Wine at the wedding

Mary had been invited to a wedding, so Jesus and some of his friends went too. Jesus was a man now. Mary knew that he had special work to do for God.

After a while, all the wine ran out. There was nothing left to drink. Mary spoke to Jesus.

'There's no wine left,' she said. 'Can you do something? The party will be spoiled.'

'Fill the jars with water,' Jesus said quietly to the

servants. 'Fill them right up to the top, then take some
to the man in charge of the feast.'

'What a surprise!' said the man who tasted it. 'This
is wonderful wine! It's the best!'

Jesus' friends were amazed. Jesus had made the
water into wine – the very best wine.

Very special friends

Jesus had some very special friends. He wanted them to help him tell people about God. He wanted them there when he helped bad people become good people, sad people become happy, and people who were ill well again.

The first four friends were fishermen: Peter, Andrew, James and John. They were busy beside the sea when he asked them to leave their nets and follow him.

Matthew, the tax collector, was counting his money when Jesus asked him to come with him.

There were twelve men altogether: Peter, Andrew, James, John, Philip, Bartholomew, Matthew, Thomas, James (yes, there were two!), Thaddeus, Simon and Judas.

Sometimes they went out two by two, telling everyone the good news.

'God loves you!' they said.

'God wants you to love him and be happy.'

'God wants you to love other people, and to be part of his special kingdom.'

The Lord's Prayer

Jesus loved God and loved to talk to him. So he told his friends how to talk to God too.

'Don't use long words that don't mean much,' Jesus

said. 'Tell God what you really feel. He wants to hear about everything that worries you.

'Say something like this: Our Father in heaven, your name is great and holy. Help us to do things that are good and right so that everyone will know who you are and your love will spread all over the world.

'Please give us all we need to eat each day, and help us to be kind to each other always. Keep us safe from harm and from doing wrong things.

'For you are the only true, wise and wonderful God and your kingdom will last for ever.'

God cares about you

The disciples were often with Jesus when he talked to people about God, his father.

'Don't worry too much about food and drink and clothes,' said Jesus. 'Look at the birds and the flowers.

'Our Father God looks after the birds and they all find food. And the wild flowers are beautiful! God has dressed them all in fine colours.

'God gives us all we need when we love him and trust him and share with each other.

'God cares for everyone, even the tiniest sparrows,' said Jesus. 'God is great and mighty and powerful but he knows about it if one falls to the ground. He knows us and cares about us too. We are safe in his strong, kind hands.'

The hole in the roof

A crowd of people had gathered in Capernaum to listen to Jesus. Four men wanted to see Jesus too. They wanted him to help their friend who couldn't walk.

But the friends couldn't get into the house. They couldn't get near the house. They couldn't see Jesus at all! So they carried their friend onto the roof.

They scraped at the roof until they made a hole. Dust and earth flew everywhere until the hole was big enough for them to let their friend down into the house – right at Jesus' feet. Jesus was happy to meet him.

'Hello,' he said. 'You can get up and go home now. Your sins are forgiven and your body is healed.'

'Who does Jesus think he is?' muttered some of the religious teachers who were in the room.

But others were amazed as the man picked up his mat and went home, a new man.

The story of two houses

Jesus told many stories to help people understand him. This was one of the stories.

'A man once built a house. He built it on good strong rock which was solid and safe,' said Jesus.

'Another man built a house too. He chose a place on the sand where it was much easier to dig.

'One day there was a great storm. The rain rained hard. The sea rose higher and higher. The wind whistled – whoo-oo! The first man's house stood firm and safe in the storm; but the second man's house was built on the shifting sand – and soon his upstairs was downstairs and his house fell to the ground.

'Build your life on the true and solid rock of my words,' Jesus said, 'so it won't tumble around your ears when troubles come.'

The storm at sea

It was the end of a long, tiring day. Jesus and his friends were sailing across Lake Galilee. It was quiet and still and soon Jesus fell asleep.

Then suddenly, a storm blew up. The wind whistled – whoo-oo – and the thunder boomed – rumble rumble – and the waves washed into the boat – slosh, slosh.

Jesus' friends were very afraid. But Jesus stayed fast asleep.

'Wake up!' they said to Jesus. 'Please! WAKE UP!'

Jesus stood up and spoke to the wind and waves.

'Hush… be quiet,' said Jesus. And the wind dropped and the waves stopped sloshing. Everything was calm. And Jesus' friends were not afraid any more.

Jesus had calmed a storm!

A very worried father

Jairus' little girl wasn't very well. She lay in bed feeling hot and tired, aching and poorly. She felt so unwell that Jairus went to find Jesus.

That day, everybody wanted Jesus to help them. There were crowds of people pushing and jostling around Jesus. So it took some time for Jairus to reach Jesus and it took some time for Jesus to come with him.

'It's too late!' a voice came through the crowd. 'Your little girl has died!'

Jairus was very upset. But Jesus went into his house with Peter and James and John.

'Trust me,' Jesus said.

Then Jairus and his wife watched as Jesus took her hand.

'Wake up, little girl,' he said.
Then Jairus' daughter opened her eyes and sat up.
'She's hungry,' said Jesus. 'Find her something to eat.'

A very big picnic

There were thousands of people out on the hillside eating a picnic!

The people had been listening to Jesus, hearing him tell them stories about God as if he really knew

what God was like. They saw him make blind people see and ill people better.

By evening everyone was hungry, as they didn't have any food.

Then a boy came to Jesus with five little bread rolls and two little fishes that his mother had given him for lunch. The boy shared all he had with Jesus.

'Thank you, God, for all you give us,' said Jesus.

Then the disciples shared out the food with everyone. It was a very big and happy picnic. And everyone somehow had enough to eat. There were even twelve baskets of food left over. It was another miracle.

The story of the good Samaritan

'How can I show God that I love him?' a man asked Jesus.

'Love God and love other people as much as you love yourself,' Jesus replied.

'Listen: there was a man who'd been walking along a lonely road when he was attacked and robbed. The man lay by the side of the road, hurting all over. He couldn't even open his eyes.

'Then the man heard footsteps coming nearer... and then going away, on the other side of the road.

'Later the man heard more footsteps coming nearer... and going away, on the other side of the road.

'Then the man heard clippetty-clop, clippetty-clop, a man on a donkey from another country, a stranger, a Samaritan!

'But the stranger did not walk away. He cleaned the man's wounds, helped him onto his donkey and took him to an inn to get better. Although he had been a stranger, the Samaritan had looked after the wounded man – he really cared about him.'

The story of the lost sheep

'God loves you like a good shepherd loves his sheep!'
Jesus once said. Then he told a story.

'Once there was a shepherd who had 100 sheep. But
one of the sheep went wandering off from the others. It
nibbled juicy grass and skipped over the hills and far away.

'The little sheep wandered further and further until it grew dark and cold and there wasn't any more juicy grass, only rocky hills and prickly bushes. The little sheep was lost.

'When the shepherd counted his sheep, he saw that there was one missing. He left his other sheep and clambered over the hillside until at last he found his little lost sheep. Then he carried him safely in his arms down the steep, rocky path.

'"I'm really happy I've found you," said the shepherd. "Let's have a party! Let's celebrate!"'

The story of the loving father

'God loves you,' said Jesus. 'God waits until you are ready to say you have made a mistake and come to say sorry. God is like the father in this story.

'The father had two sons. The younger son left home taking his share of his father's money. Suddenly

he was rich! He spent his money on all sorts of things – until suddenly he'd spent it all!

'Now he was so poor that he had to work on a pig farm. He was so poor that he wanted to eat the pigs' food! So he decided to go home to his father.

'His father saw him coming from a long way off. He was overjoyed to see him.

'"I'm really sorry," said the young man to his father. "I've been selfish and greedy and…"

'But his father was already calling to his servants.

'"My son has come home!" he shouted. "Bring my best cloak, a ring for his finger and shoes for his feet. Let's celebrate!"'

The man who couldn't see

Bartimaeus was blind. He could smell the flowers but he couldn't see them. He could hear the wind rustling in the leaves but he couldn't see the trees. He could feel the hot sun but he couldn't see the blue sky.

Bartimaeus was blind, and so he could not work. He sat by the roadside, day after day, begging for money.

One day Bartimaeus heard the sound of a happy crowd coming along the road. When Bartimaeus found out that Jesus was coming, he called out.

'Jesus!' called Bartimaeus. 'Help me!'

'Who's there?' said Jesus.

Then kind hands helped him to his feet and led him to Jesus.

When Jesus knew that Bartimaeus wanted to see, he healed him. Suddenly Bartimaeus could see the flowers

and the trees and the blue sky. And he could see
Jesus.

Bartimaeus thanked God. Then he followed Jesus
along the road.

Zacchaeus meets Jesus

Zacchaeus had lots of money. But he had not always been a kind man or a good man and he didn't

have many friends. He didn't really have any friends. People said he was a cheat.

Zacchaeus wanted to see Jesus but so did lots of other people – and Zacchaeus was too small to see over their heads. So he climbed up a fig tree and looked down on all the people.

He saw Jesus walking along the road and saw him coming closer and closer until… Jesus was looking up at Zacchaeus!

'Come down,' said Jesus. 'I'd like to come to your house today.'

Zacchaeus slithered down through the branches as fast as a grown man could. He took Jesus to his house.

'You're my friend now,' said Zacchaeus to Jesus. 'I'll give money back to anyone I have cheated, and share what I have left with the poor.'

Then Zacchaeus felt very, very happy.

Jesus rides a donkey

Jesus and his friends were on their way to the big city of Jerusalem.

'There's a little donkey in that village,' Jesus said to his friends one day. 'No one has ever sat on its back. It's young and wild, but I want you to bring it to me.'

Carefully, Jesus' special friends fetched the donkey. They put their coats over the donkey's back and helped Jesus climb on. Then Jesus rode to Jerusalem.

It was all very noisy and exciting. Crowds of people welcomed him into the city. Lots of men, women and children followed too.

They threw their coats down on the road in front of Jesus. They threw palm branches in front of him. They cheered and waved and shouted.

'Hurrah!' everyone cried out.

'Praise God! Hosanna!'
'Praise the King of peace!'
'Praise King Jesus!'

The woman who loved God

Jesus and his friends were near the temple.

People were dropping money into a box. Some rich people made sure others were looking as they put LOTS of money in the box.

Then a poor woman came along. She didn't look to see who was watching. She didn't care what people thought of her at all. She came because she loved God. Quietly, she dropped two little coins into the box.

'Look,' said Jesus to his disciples. 'This woman has been really generous. The rich people gave a lot of money but they still have lots of money left. This woman is all alone in the world. She has hardly enough to eat yet she has given everything she has. She has given far more than anyone else because she loves God.'

Jesus prays in the garden

Later in the week, Jesus and his friends ate together. Jesus was thoughtful.

He offered them bread and said it was like his broken body; he offered them wine and said it was like his blood. Jesus told them how important it was that they take care of each other.

After supper, they went to a garden of olive trees and Jesus prayed.

'I will do whatever you want, Father God,' said Jesus. 'But please help me.'

Jesus knew that Judas had gone to tell Jesus' enemies where he was so they could arrest him secretly.

When Jesus went back to his friends, he found they had fallen asleep while he was praying. Jesus felt sad and lonely.

Suddenly there were torches and lights in the darkness. Judas appeared out of the darkness. He greeted Jesus, so

the soldiers knew who he was. The soldiers
arrested Jesus and marched him away.

Three crosses on a hillside

Everyone who knew Jesus was shocked at what happened next.

Jesus was taken for questioning. No one really knew what he was there for. They knew he had done nothing wrong. But his enemies wanted him out of the way.

Then Jesus, who had healed people, helped them and been kind to them, was crucified on a cross on a hillside between two thieves.

Jesus asked God, his father, to forgive the soldiers and the thieves and everyone in the world for everything they'd ever done wrong. Jesus was dying for them.

Then there was an earthquake and darkness in the middle of the day. Jesus took his last breath and died.

A sad garden

A kind man called Joseph carried Jesus' dead body to his own beautiful garden with the help of a man called Nicodemus.

Scents of flowers and damp grass and leafy trees drifted across the evening air. The garden felt grey and quiet and still.

They buried Jesus in a quiet, dark cave. Then they rolled a very big, heavy stone across the doorway.

No one could get in. No one could get out.

Jesus' mother was very sad. Jesus' friend John was very sad. They looked after each other. All Jesus' friends were very, very sad. They knew they would never see Jesus again.

It was the saddest day there had ever been.

A happy garden

Early on Sunday morning, some women who were friends of Jesus took sweet-smelling spices to the garden where he had been buried. But

they found that the big, heavy stone had been rolled away. The cave was empty!

Two shining angels sat beside the cave.

'Jesus isn't here,' said the angel. 'Be happy! Go and tell everyone – he is alive again!'

The women ran to tell Peter and Jesus' other friends, but they could not understand what had happened.

Peter and John ran to the garden – and saw the empty tomb for themselves, but they could not understand what had happened.

Mary Magdalene stayed by the empty cave, crying. She could not understand what had happened.

'Mary!' said a kind voice behind her.

Mary turned. She knew that voice. It was Jesus! She was so happy.

Mary ran back to Jesus' other friends and told them, 'Jesus is alive! I have seen him!'

It was the happiest day there had ever been!

Two friends along the road

That very same evening, a man called Cleopas and his friend were walking to a nearby village. They talked together sadly, because Jesus had died.

A stranger joined them.

'Why are you so sad?' asked the stranger.

'Haven't you heard?' they answered. 'We're sad because Jesus – the best person ever – has been crucified. He died on Friday.'

Then the man walked with them. He talked and they listened. He told them wonderful, exciting things about God.

'Come and have supper with us,' said the friends when they reached home. 'It's getting dark.'

The stranger went into their house and broke some bread – and suddenly the friends knew who he was. The stranger who had walked with them was Jesus!

Jesus and Thomas

Jesus really was alive again.

'I can't believe it,' said Thomas. 'I won't believe it unless I see Jesus myself.'

Jesus had come to see his friends on Sunday when they were together in a locked room.

He had even stayed for supper.

But Thomas had not been there. He had missed him.

'But it's true,' said his friends. 'We've seen him. We've spoken to him. Jesus really is alive!'

A week later Jesus came to see his friends again. This time Thomas was there too.

'Peace be with you,' said Jesus. Then he turned to Thomas. 'Look at me,' Jesus said. 'Touch me. Now do you believe I am real – that I am alive?'

Thomas looked… and looked… and then he knew that it was Jesus.

'Jesus!' gasped Thomas. 'It really is you. You are my Lord and my God.'

Breakfast by the lake

One night, Peter and his friends were out in their boat, fishing on Lake Galilee.

They fished and fished and fished all night, but they didn't catch any fish at all.

Just as the sun was rising, they heard a man's voice from the water's edge.

'Have you caught anything?' called the man.

'No, nothing,' they replied gloomily. 'Not even the tiniest, teeniest tiddler.'

'Put out your net on the other side,' the man shouted back.

So the friends put out their net on the other side of the boat. Then the net was full of so many fish that the friends could hardly pull it in!

'It's Jesus!' they said.

Peter jumped into the water and waded to the beach. And there was Jesus, making breakfast.

The friends dragged in the net, full of wiggling, wriggling fish.

'Come and eat,' said Jesus, and they all ate fish and bread together on the beach.

Jesus goes back to heaven

Jesus and his special friends stood talking to each other on a hillside.

'Will everyone soon know you are our real king?' his friends asked Jesus.

'Not quite yet,' smiled Jesus kindly. 'One day. I'm going back to heaven first. I'm going back to my father. But I want you to tell other people that the secret of being happy is to love God and be kind to everyone else. I will always be with you to help you.'

As Jesus spoke, a cloud came down the hillside. When the cloud moved away, Jesus had gone.

While his friends stared up at the sky, two angels stood beside them.

'Don't worry – one day, Jesus will come back again,' they said.

Wind and fire

It was a feast day, a festival called Pentecost. Jesus' special friends were all together.

Then, suddenly, there was a strong wind, a strong and mighty rushing wind that filled the whole house.

Then there were little flames, safe, bright little flames that didn't burn, but touched everyone's heads.

Everyone felt excited and happy.

'I want to tell God how much I love him!' said one.

'God loves me! I can feel how much he loves me,' said another.

Then they realised they could speak languages they had never learned – they would be able to tell people from other countries about Jesus in their own language!

A big crowd gathered outside the house from many different countries.

'What's going on?' said the people in the crowd.

Then Peter went to talk to them. He told them about Jesus, who was God's son, come to save them.

'God's Spirit has come,' he said. 'It's as if Jesus himself were here with us, helping us in all we do.'

The Holy Spirit helps

God helped Peter and John and his other friends to be bold and brave.

Peter spoke to all the crowds of people.

'Jesus is God's Son,' said Peter. 'He loves you and died for you. He is Lord of all the world. He is King of the whole earth. Stop doing bad things. Tell him you are sorry. He will forgive you.'

A lot of people listened to Peter. They learned about God together. They prayed to God and praised him together. They had meals together. They cared and shared together.

God helped them heal people who were ill, just as Jesus had done. Jesus' friends weren't afraid any more. They knew that God was always with them, although he was invisible, like the wind.

Saul's new name

Aman called Saul loved God, but he hated the new Christians.

'You're all wrong,' he said. 'Stop telling people about Jesus!'

He was so sure he was right, he helped put the Christians in prison. He even went to a city called Damascus to stop people following Jesus. But on the way something amazing happened. Saul met Jesus.

Saul was surrounded by a light so bright that he couldn't see. He fell to the ground. Then Saul heard a voice.

'Why are you hurting my friends, Saul?' said Jesus. 'When you're cruel to the people who love me, you're being cruel to me too.'

Now Saul knew that Jesus was alive. Jesus was God's Son. Saul wanted Jesus to be his friend too. Saul joined the Christians and started to tell everyone about Jesus. Now they called him Paul.

Paul was just as keen to help the Christians as he had been to stop them. News spread everywhere about God's love and forgiveness and soon people in many places were baptised.

Peter goes to prison

Peter told everyone about how much God loved them. He told them that Jesus had died and was alive again so that everyone could be God's friend.

But some people didn't like what Peter said. Peter was put in prison and chained up between two guards.

'Let's pray for Peter,' said Peter's friends. Together, in Mary's house, they prayed.

Peter was sleeping in the prison when God answered their prayers. An angel came to Peter's prison cell.

'Wake up!' said the angel. 'Follow me.'

The chains fell from Peter's wrists. Peter followed the angel out of the prison. The prison guards didn't stop him and the big iron gates swung open for him. Peter went straight to Mary's house and knocked on the door.

A girl called Rhoda answered.

'It's Peter! It's Peter!' she shouted. She was so excited, she forgot to let him in!

Peter knocked again. This time everyone rushed to the door. Then they thanked God for answering their prayers.

Paul is shipwrecked!

Paul and his friends made journeys to many places to tell people about Jesus.

Sometimes their journeys were dangerous. Sometimes Paul was put in prison.

'I want to go to Rome to see the Emperor,' said Paul. 'He can decide whether I can go on telling people about Jesus.'

So Paul and his friends sailed to Rome.

On the way there was a storm. The ship rocked up and down in the big waves. But God took care of Paul and his friends.

'God will look after us. We won't drown,' said Paul. And they didn't drown.

The next morning the boat hit a big sandbank near the island of Malta. Everyone on the boat had to swim to shore. People there welcomed the shipwrecked sailors, and looked after them until it was safe for them to sail again to Rome.

Paul told the people in Malta about Jesus.

When he arrived in Rome, he was allowed to stay in a house and write to all his friends, teaching them about Jesus, even though he was a long way from them.

Paul writes thank-you letters

Paul wrote letters to Christians in some of the places he had visited.

He wrote to tell them that he often thought about them and asked God to look after them.

He wrote to thank them for making him welcome.

He wrote to tell them that God loved them so much that he had sent Jesus to help them.

He wrote to remind them that all people – even Paul himself – was in need of God's forgiveness. No one was perfect.

He wrote to remind them to love God, not just today but every day.

He wrote to remind them to be kind to each other, and to share what they had with other people.

No more tears

After Jesus had risen from the dead, his friend John was sent to live on an island called Patmos.

While he was there, he wrote to the new Christian churches too.

'God is pure, and God is holy.

'God is good, and God is true and fair.

'Holy, holy, holy is the Lord God Almighty.

'He will live and reign for ever.

'All the angels and every creature will worship him for ever and ever.'

Then God gave John a dream in which he heard loud trumpets in the starry skies. He saw a sparkling, flowing river and tree-lined streets. He imagined a wonderful heavenly city shining like the sun.

It was a holy city, where no one would be hurt again and there would be no more pain. No one would cry and no one would ever die again. It was a wonderful place where everyone who lived there could see God living among them.

'Lord Jesus, come and be with everyone,' said John.

Graces

Thank you for the world so sweet.
Thank you for the food we eat,
Thank you for the birds that sing.
Thank you, God for everything.

Edith Rutter Leatham

All good gifts around us
are sent from heaven above.
Then thank the Lord,
O thank the Lord,
for all his love.

Matthias Claudius

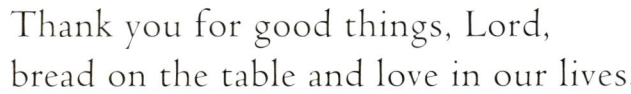

Thank you for good things, Lord,
bread on the table and love in our lives.

Based on I Chronicles 29:11-14

The eagles give thanks for the mountains,
the fish give thanks for the sea,
we give thanks for our blessings
and for what we're about to receive.

A native American prayer

For this and all his many mercies,
God's holy name be blessed and praised.

Traditional

Bedtime Prayers

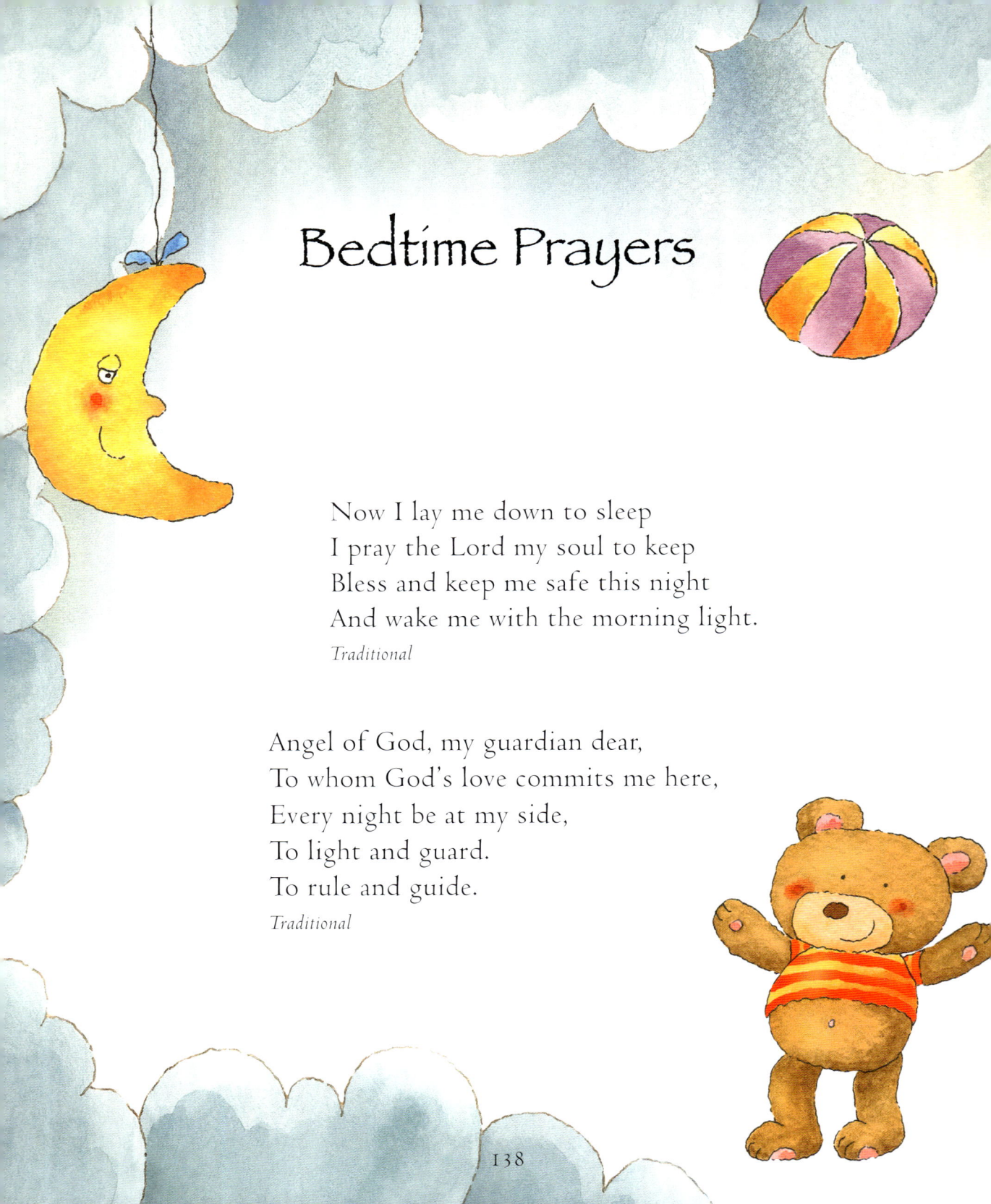

Now I lay me down to sleep
I pray the Lord my soul to keep
Bless and keep me safe this night
And wake me with the morning light.

Traditional

Angel of God, my guardian dear,
To whom God's love commits me here,
Every night be at my side,
To light and guard.
To rule and guide.

Traditional

Be near me, Lord Jesus,
I ask you to stay
Close by me for ever
And love me, I pray.
Bless all the dear children
In your tender care
And take us to heaven to live with you there.

John T. McFarland (Away in a Manger)

Stay, dear Lord,
with those who wake,
or watch, or weep tonight.
Let angels guard those who sleep.
Take care of those who are ill,
give rest to those who are weary,
help the dying,
and give hope to the suffering.

Based on a prayer by St Augustine

Blessings

May the Lord bless us and watch over us.
May the Lord make his face to shine upon us
and be gracious to us.
May the Lord look kindly on us
and give us peace;
and the blessing of God almighty,
the Father, Son and Holy Spirit,
be with us and remain with us now and every day.

Based on Numbers 6:24-26

May God greatly bless us with his kindness;
with fresh, flowing waters of kindness.
May God greatly bless us with his peace;
with still, quiet waters of peace.
May God greatly bless us with his love;
with deep, thirst-quenching waters of love
now and always.

Based on Jude 2

Published 2018 by Authentic Media Ltd,
PO Box 6326, Bletchley, Milton Keynes, MK1 9GG
Conforms to EN71 and AS/NZS ISO 8124

Copyright © this edition 2018 Anno Domini Publishing
Original Copyright © 2012 Anno Domini Publishing
www.ad-publishing.com
Text copyright © 2012 Lizzie Ribbons
Illustrations copyright © 2012 Paola Bertolini Grudina

Publishing Director: Annette Reynolds
Art Director: Gerald Rogers
Pre-production Manager: Doug Hewitt

Printed and bound in China